FLIGHT 19
LOST IN THE
BERMUDA TRIANGLE

BY CHRIS BOWMAN
ILLUSTRATION BY TATE YOTTER
COLOR BY GERARDO SANDOVAL

BELLWETHER MEDIA · MINNEAPOLIS, MN

STRAY FROM REGULAR READS WITH BLACK SHEEP BOOKS. FEEL A RUSH WITH EVERY READ!

Library of Congress Cataloging-in-Publication Data

Names: Bowman, Chris, 1990- author.
Title: Flight 19 : Lost in the Bermuda Triangle / by Chris Bowman.
Other titles: Flight nineteen
Description: Minneapolis, MN : Bellwether Media, Inc., 2020. | Series: Black Sheep: Paranormal Mysteries | Includes
   bibliographical references and index.
Identifiers: LCCN 2019003840 (print) | LCCN 2019018242 (ebook) | ISBN 9781618916662 (ebook) |
   ISBN 9781644870945 (hardcover : alk. paper) | ISBN 9781618917324 (pbk. : alk. paper)
Subjects: LCSH: Bermuda Triangle–Juvenile literature. | Aircraft accidents–Bermuda Triangle–Juvenile literature.
Classification: LCC G558 (ebook) | LCC G558 .B68 2020 (print) | DDC 001.94–dc23
LC record available at https://lccn.loc.gov/2019003840

This edition first published in 2020 by Bellwether Media, Inc.

Editor: Christina Leaf   Designer: Andrea Schneider

Printed in the United States of America, North Mankato, MN.

TABLE OF CONTENTS

Red text identifies
historical quotes.

December 5, 1945:
The pilots and crew of Flight 19 prepare for their training **mission** in Fort Lauderdale, Florida. The five TBM Avenger planes will fly east to practice dropping **torpedoes**. Then they will fly north before returning home.

Captain Powers, are the planes ready?

They're loaded up and fully fueled!

Lieutenant Charles Taylor leads Flight 19. He is in charge of four other pilots and nine crew members.

Good. Looks like a great day to fly.

Flight 19 will fly east for about 140 miles. Then it will head north for around 85 miles before turning back to the base.

GRAND BAHAMA

FORT LAUDERDALE

HEN AND CHICKEN SHOALS

N
W E
S

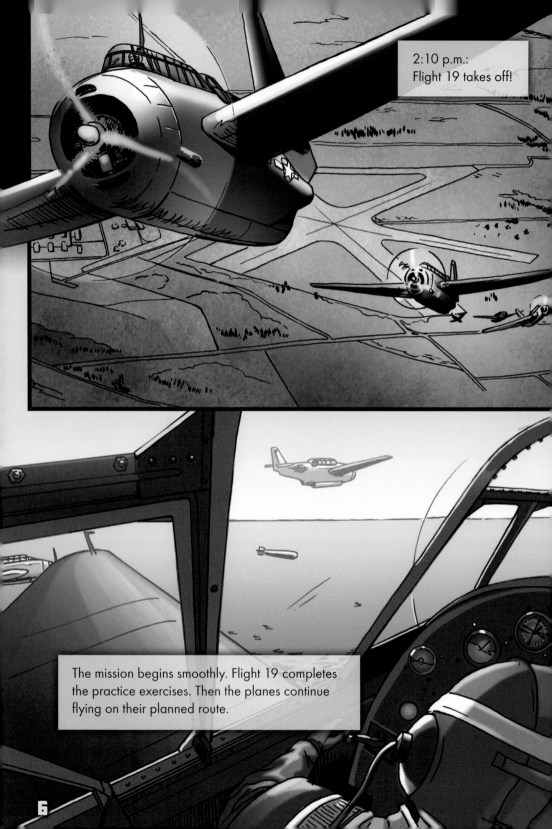

2:10 p.m.:
Flight 19 takes off!

The mission begins smoothly. Flight 19 completes
the practice exercises. Then the planes continue
flying on their planned route.

But soon, their luck runs out.

3:40 p.m.:
Back in Fort Lauderdale, Lieutenant Robert Cox overhears confused messages on his radio.

Captain Powers, what is your **compass** reading?

I don't know where we are. We must have got lost after that last turn.

Operation Radio, it sounds like a boat or some planes are lost.

Roger that, Lieutenant Cox.

3:45 p.m.: Lieutenant Cox reports what he has heard to Operation Radio in the Fort Lauderdale Control Tower.

Then Cox tries to contact Flight 19.

Plane or boat calling "Powers," please identify yourself so someone can help you.

FLORIDA

FORT
LAUDERDALE

★ TAYLOR'S
PROBABLE
LOCATION

TAYLOR'S
ASSUMED LOCATION

BAHAMAS

Lieutenant Taylor thinks that something has gone terribly wrong. Instead of flying east and north, he believes Flight 19 has gone south and west to the Florida Keys.

Fly up the coast until you get to Miami, then Fort Lauderdale is 20 miles further.

What is your present **altitude**? I will fly south and meet you.

I know where I am now. I'm at 2,300 feet. Don't come after me.

Roger. I'm coming to meet you anyhow.

Your **transmissions** are fading. Something is wrong.

Suddenly, Lieutenant Cox loses his connection with Taylor. He tries other radio **frequencies** but is unable to contact Flight 19 again. He returns to Fort Lauderdale.

4:25 p.m.:
After losing touch with Cox, Flight 19 connects with Port Everglades in Fort Lauderdale. This unit focuses on air-sea rescues.

Can you read us?

Affirmative. We have just passed over a small island. We have no other land in sight.

Does anyone in the area have a radar screen that could pick us up?

Port Everglades suggests having another pilot in Flight 19 with working compasses guide the plane back to the **mainland**. Meanwhile, the unit prepares a search plane to look for Flight 19.

Taylor agrees, but none of the other pilots know where they are.

One of the planes in the flight thinks that if we went west we could hit land.

4:45 p.m.:
Soon after, Flight 19 changes its plans.

FLIGHT 19'S
POSSIBLE ROUTE

We will fly northeast for 45 minutes.

Then we will fly north to make sure we are not over the **Gulf** of Mexico.

BAHAMAS

In Fort Lauderdale, Lieutenant Commander Don Poole hears Flight 19's new plan.

Port Everglades, do you copy? Tell Flight 19 to continue west.

5:00 p.m.:
Poole hears a message over the radio. But he does not know who sends it.

If we would just fly west, we would get home.

Nevertheless, Flight 19 continues northeast.

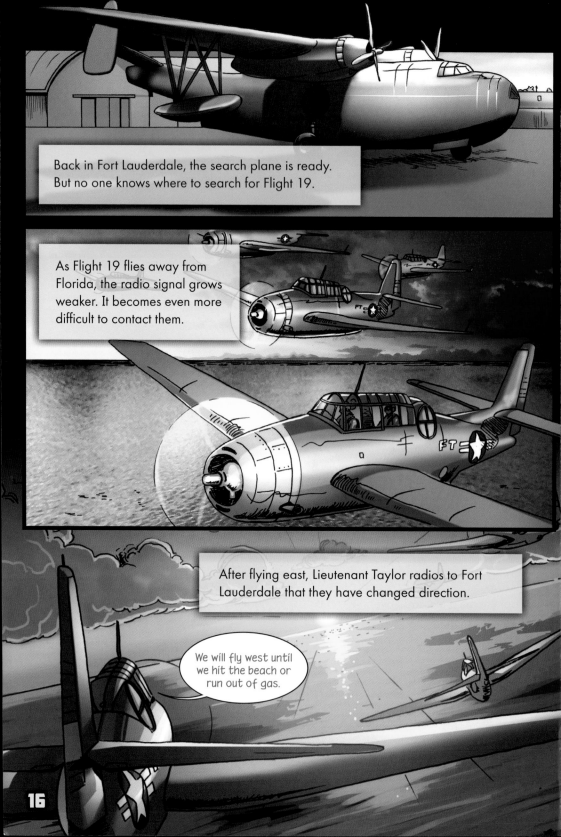

Back in Fort Lauderdale, the search plane is ready. But no one knows where to search for Flight 19.

As Flight 19 flies away from Florida, the radio signal grows weaker. It becomes even more difficult to contact them.

After flying east, Lieutenant Taylor radios to Fort Lauderdale that they have changed direction.

We will fly west until we hit the beach or run out of gas.

5:22 p.m.:
The pilots also prepare for the worst.

6:00 p.m.:
Suddenly, Flight 19's location is picked up over radio. The control towers have an idea where the planes are.

APPROXIMATE LOCATION OF FLIGHT 19

When the first man gets down to 10 gallons of gas we will all land in the water together. Does everyone understand that?

7:04 p.m.:
Fort Lauderdale gets one more transmission from Flight 19. Then all they hear is **static**.

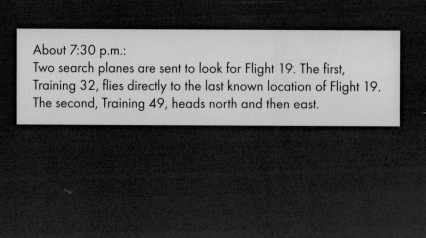

About 7:30 p.m.:
Two search planes are sent to look for Flight 19. The first,
Training 32, flies directly to the last known location of Flight 19.
The second, Training 49, heads north and then east.

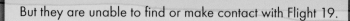

But they are unable to find or make contact with Flight 19.

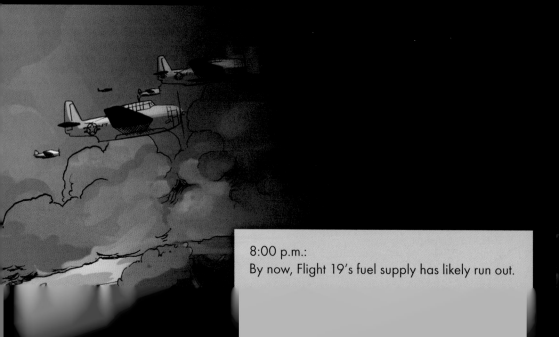

8:00 p.m.:
By now, Flight 19's fuel supply has likely run out.

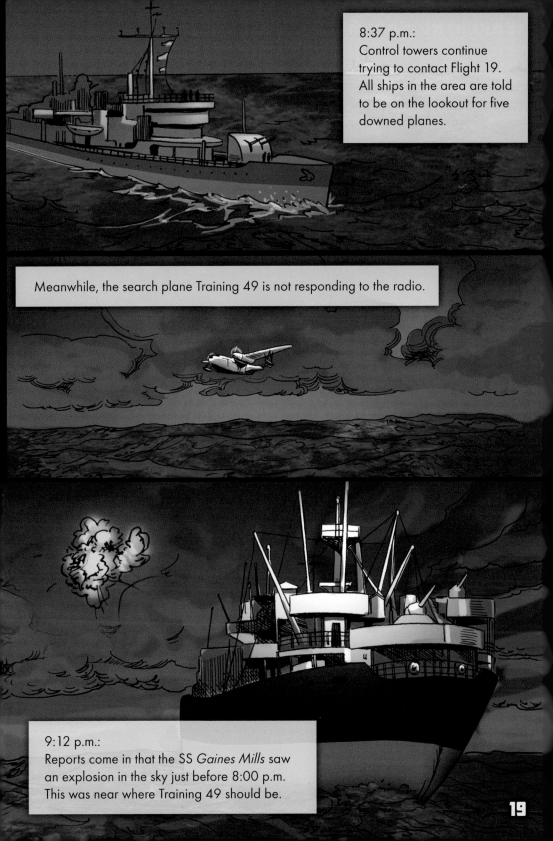

8:37 p.m.:
Control towers continue
trying to contact Flight 19.
All ships in the area are told
to be on the lookout for five
downed planes.

Meanwhile, the search plane Training 49 is not responding to the radio.

9:12 p.m.:
Reports come in that the SS *Gaines Mills* saw
an explosion in the sky just before 8:00 p.m.
This was near where Training 49 should be.

SEARCHING FOR ANSWERS

After searching for Flight 19, Training 32 looks for Training 49. But there is no trace of the plane.

Soon, the Army, Navy, and Coast Guard begin one of the biggest search and rescue efforts in history.

Hundreds of planes and ships search more than 200,000 square miles of the Atlantic Ocean.

Search crews also fly over Florida in search of **debris**. Nothing is ever found.

The fates of Flight 19 and Training 49 have never been fully explained. Other ships and planes have also had strange experiences or gone missing in the area. The mysteries of the Bermuda Triangle continue.

Theories Behind the Disappearance

- The Navy's explanation is that four of the pilots in Flight 19 were training. The instructor, Taylor, had broken compasses so he could not lead the planes home.

- Many people say that humans are to blame for accidents or disappearances in the Bermuda Triangle. Pilots without experience are more likely to make mistakes.

- Some people think that alien spacecraft fly over the Bermuda Triangle. They say spacecraft disrupt radios and navigation instruments.

- Others think that weather is to blame. The search planes reported high winds and choppy water. Weather can change quickly in this area of the ocean.

- Some theories focus on the search planes. The search planes were Martin Mariners, understood to be unsafe. It only took a spark for these planes to catch fire and explode.

Timeline
December 5, 1945

2:10 p.m.:
Flight 19 takes off

6:00 p.m.: Flight 19's location is detected north of the Bahamas

3:40 p.m.: The first confused messages from Flight 19 are received in Fort Lauderdale

Glossary

affirmative—a statement of agreement

altitude—the height above sea level

compass—an instrument that uses magnets to determine direction

debris—the scattered pieces of something broken down or destroyed

frequencies—settings on radios at which people can communicate

gulf—part of an ocean or sea that extends into land

mainland—a large region of an area; a mainland is often contrasted with islands.

mission—a task that a person or a group is charged with completing

radar—a system that uses radio waves to find and track planes, ships, and other objects

static—noise from a radio due to electrical interference

torpedoes—weapons dropped from planes that are designed to explode upon reaching a target

transmissions—communications sent through a radio

7:30 p.m.: Two search planes are sent

9:12 p.m.: Reports come in that an explosion has been seen near Training 49's location

7:04 p.m.: The last transmission from Flight 19

8:00 p.m.: The calculated time that Flight 19 would have run out of fuel

To Learn More

AT THE LIBRARY

azynka, Kitson. *History's Mysteries: Curious Clues, Cold Cases, and Puzzles from the Past*. Washington, D.C.: National Geographic, 2017.

Polinsky, Paige V. *The Bermuda Triangle*. Minneapolis, Minn.: Bellwether Media, 2020.

Richard, Orlin. *Investigating the Bermuda Triangle*. New York, N.Y.: AV2 by Weigl, 2020.

ON THE WEB

FACTSURFER

Factsurfer.com gives you a safe, fun way to find more information.

1. Go to www.factsurfer.com
2. Enter "Flight 19" into the search box and click 🔍.
3. Select your book cover to see a list of related web sites.

INDEX